in Science

ALL ABOUT ANIMALS

Fish

JOANNE MATTERN

PERFECTION LEARNING®

Editorial Director: Susan C. Thies
Editor: Mary L. Bush
Design Director: Randy Messer
Book Design: Randy Messer, Tobi Cunningham
Cover Design: Michael A. Aspengren

A special thanks to the following for his scientific review of the book:
Paul Pistek, Instructor of Biological Sciences,
North Iowa Area Community College

Image Credits:

©Handout/Reuters/CORBIS: p. 5 (bottom right); ©Brandon D. Cole/CORBIS: p. 6; ©Jeffrey L. Rotman/
CORBIS: p. 11 (bottom); ©Clouds Hill Imaging Ltd./CORBIS: p. 13 (bottom); ©Bob Rowan; Progressive
Image/CORBIS: p. 28; ©Jeff Rotman/Photo Researchers, Inc.: p. 23

Photos.com: chapter title bars (third image), p. 22 (top); Corel: front and back cover, chapter title bars
(second and fourth images), pp. 3, 4 (background), 7 (bottom), 8, 9, 10 (top left, bottom right), 11 (top),
12, 14 (top left, bottom right), 15, 16, 17, 18, 20, 21 (bottom), 22 (bottom), 25, 26, 29, 30, 31, 32;
Randy Messer: pp. 5 (left center), 10 (bottom left), 19, 24; Corbis Royalty Free: chapter title bars
(first and fifth images), p. 5 (upper right); Clipart: p.14 (bottom left)

For information, contact
Perfection Learning® Corporation
1000 North Second Avenue, P.O. Box 500
Logan, Iowa 51546-0500.
Phone: 1-800-831-4190
Fax: 1-800-543-2745
perfectionlearning.com

4 5 6 7 8 9 PP 18 17 16

PB ISBN-13: 978-0-7891-6613-5
RLB ISBN-13: 978-0-7569-4637-1

Table of Contents

Introducing
Fish

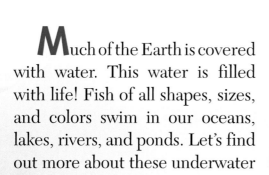

Much of the Earth is covered with water. This water is filled with life! Fish of all shapes, sizes, and colors swim in our oceans, lakes, rivers, and ponds. Let's find out more about these underwater creatures.

Fishy Facts

More than 25,000 different **species** of fish make their home underwater. Fish are vertebrates, or animals with backbones. In fact, fish make up about half of all vertebrate species.

The majority of fish are cold-blooded. That means their body temperature depends on the temperature around them. Since fish live in water, the temperature of the water affects their body temperature. Fish that live in cold water have lower body temperatures than fish that live in warm water.

They're Getting Warmer . . .

Tunas and some shark species have body temperatures higher than water temperatures.

Great white shark

Most fish have several special body parts suited for life in the water. **Gills** help fish get oxygen out of water. **Scales** cover fish to protect them. **Fins** move fish through the water.

And, of course, all fish live in water. Certain members of other animal groups also live in the water. For example, mammals such as seals, birds such as pelicans, and reptiles such as turtles spend all or much of their time in the water. However, *all* fish live in the water.

Extreme Fish

• The largest fish is the whale shark. This fish can grow to more than 40 feet long.

Whale shark

• The smallest fish is the stout infantfish. This tiny fish is less than a quarter of an inch long. That's about the same length as the width of a pencil!

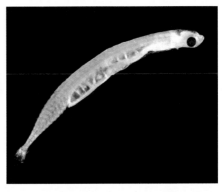

Stout infantfish

Fish Families

Fish are divided into three groups. Most fish are bony fish. They have skeletons made of bone. Most bony fish are covered in scales and have pairs of fins.

Cartilaginous fish are the second group. The skeletons of these fish are made of **cartilage**. Cartilage is softer and more flexible than bone. Sharks, skates, and rays are cartilaginous fish.

The third type of fish is jawless fish. As you might have guessed, these fish have no jaws. They also don't have pairs of fins like other fish. The skeletons of jawless fish are made of cartilage. There are only two kinds of jawless fish living today. They are the hagfish and the lamprey.

Hagfish

Body Basics

Torpedo-shaped fish race through the waves. Flatfish lie on the bottom of the sea. Fish with snakelike bodies wriggle through the water. Puffed-up fish look like round water balloons. Despite these differences in appearance, most fish share some common body basics that make them suited to life in the water.

Spotted flatfish

caudal fin

dorsal fin

anal fin

pelvic fin

pectoral fin

Nassau grouper

Built for Swimming

A fish's body is designed for swimming. The head is smaller than the body and usually comes to a rounded point. The body is curved and smooth. This unique shape allows water to flow over fish so they can move through the water quickly and easily.

Most fish have fins. Fins help a fish swim and keep its balance. A fin is made of a thin **membrane** stretched over rods called *spines*. The fin on top of a fish's body is called the *dorsal fin*. A fish can have two different types of bottom fins. A bottom fin toward the front is a pelvic fin. One toward the back is an anal fin. Fins on the sides are pectoral fins. A fish's tail is actually a fin too. It's called a *caudal fin*. Not all fish have all types of fins. The number of fins on a fish varies with each species.

Fish use their muscles to move through the water. They wave or bend their bodies to propel themselves forward. They also use their fins and tails to move, steer, and balance.

Eels can swim backward as well as forward.

Viper moray eel

The majority of fish swim at speeds of about five to ten miles per hour. The fastest fish are tunas and sharks. These fish can race through the water in short spurts at speeds of up to 50 mph.

Most fish swim in a horizontal position. Sea horses and pipefish are among the exceptions. These fish have rings of hard bone around their bodies. This makes their bodies very stiff and holds them upright when they swim.

Swim bladders help fish move up and down in the water. A swim bladder is a sac inside the body that can fill up with air like a balloon. It is also called an *air bladder* or *gas bladder*. When a fish wants to move upward, it draws in more air. This will make the fish "lighter" so it rises in the water. When a fish wants to swim deeper in the water, it lets out some of the air.

Reef shark

Sharks, skates, and rays don't have a swim bladder. Instead they store large quantities of liver oil in their bodies to help them float.

Blue-spotted stingray

A Breath of Water?

Like humans, fish take in oxygen and circulate it through their bodies. However, fish get their oxygen from water instead of air. To do this, they have gills instead of lungs.

Gills under the operculum

Gills are tiny flaps held up by bony arches. They are found behind a fish's mouth. Most gills sit under a bony covering called the *operculum*. As a fish swims, water flows into its mouth and over the gills. Tiny blood vessels in the gills absorb oxygen from the water. Then the water flows out of the gills through a slit under the operculum.

Air Breathers

Some fish can get oxygen from the air when necessary. The mudskipper can absorb oxygen through its wet skin so it can "take a walk" on land for short periods of time. Eels can take in oxygen in the air through their body surface. Lungfish actually have one or two lungs that can draw in oxygen from the air.

Mudskipper

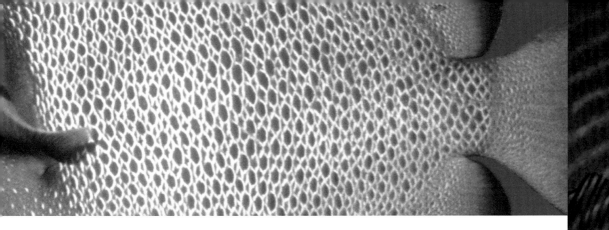

A Fish in Shining Scales

A covering of tough scales protects most fish from harm. Others, like the armored catfish, have hard outer coverings or plates. Fish without scales often have a leathery outer skin or a slimy coating that serves as protection. Catfish, clingfish, hagfish, and lampreys are a few fish that don't have scales.

That Makes Sense!

Most fish have good eyesight. Many have big eyes that stick out either in front or on the sides. These bulging eyes help the fish get a clear view of the area around them. Flatfish spend their lives lying on the bottom of the ocean, so they have both eyes on the same side of their body. A few fish, such as the four-eyed fish, can see images both above and below the water at the same time.

Flatfish

11

Fish don't have eyelids. That means they sleep with their eyes open!

Queen angelfish

Sound travels faster in water than in air. Fish have ears inside their bodies to detect this sound. Some fish use their air bladders to increase sound reception.

Fish use smell to locate food. Eels, salmon, and sharks have especially strong senses of smell. A shark can smell a tiny amount of blood in the water from a great distance. This ability leads sharks to injured **prey**.

Fish have taste buds in their mouths just like humans. Some species even have taste buds on the outside of their bodies. They can use these taste buds to identify foods before eating them. Catfish and goatfish have whiskers called *barbels* that can taste.

Fish have senses that land animals do not. Fish can feel changes in water pressure. Some can sense changes in the electrical field around them if **predators** or prey are moving nearby.

Fish also have a special sense organ called the *lateral line*. The lateral line runs down the center of a fish's body. It helps the fish sense when a predator or obstacle is near. The lateral line also helps fish that swim in large groups to turn and move together in the water.

Whitetipped reef shark

Cycles of Life 3

Fish families are like all other animal families. Fish parents have babies that grow up and have their own babies. This keeps the cycle of life going.

An "Egg"ceptional Beginning

Most fish hatch from eggs. Some fish, such as the cod, produce several million tiny eggs at one time. Other fish, such as sharks, lay just a few eggs at a time.

The majority of fish lay eggs each year of their adult lives. Other fish, such as salmon, die soon after laying eggs once.

Fish build different kinds of nests for their eggs. Trout make a hole in the bottom of a river. Then they lay their eggs in the hole and cover them with small stones. Sticklebacks build nests out of weeds. Skates lay each of their eggs in a tough case called a *purse*.

Brown trout eggs

13

Most fish don't protect their
eggs. They just lay them and go.
A few fish, however, do protect
their eggs. Male sea horses and
pipefish, for example, carry the
eggs in a pouch on their stomachs
until they hatch. Tilapia mothers
and catfish fathers hold their eggs
in their mouths.

Just Like Mom and Dad

Some fish don't lay eggs.
Swordtails, guppies, and some
shark species are among the fish
that give birth to live young.

Swordtail

Life as a Fish

When a group of fish hatch,
they are called *fry*. Many fish
fry don't live long enough to
become adults. They are eaten by
predators when they're young.

Those that do survive grow up
quickly. It doesn't take long before
they look like their parents. Fish
are considered adults when they
are able to **reproduce**.

The life span of fish varies
greatly. A variety of fish, such
as bettas and killifish, only live
for a few years. Other fish
species live much longer.
Some sturgeons and
groupers can live
for more than
50 years.

Nassua
grouper

14

Happy Birthday to You

One way that scientists can tell the age of a fish is by counting growth rings on its scales.

Fish may live alone or in groups. Large groups of fish are called *schools*. Staying together keeps fish safe and can make finding food easier. Some fish, such as snappers and rockfish, may live in schools when they're younger and then go off on their own when they get older.

Hawkfish feeding on red gorgonian sea fan

Swimming with the Big Fish

Fish spend much of their time defending themselves against predators. **Camouflage** can help a fish stay safe. The coloring of some fish helps them blend into the environment around them. For example, the bright red lines on the tartan hawkfish might make you think it would stand out in the water. However, they actually camouflage the fish when it swims among the red gorgonian sea fans growing in its **habitat**.

Other fish look like parts of their habitats. Sea dragons look like seaweed. Stonefish look like rocks.

A variety of fish have special body parts or behaviors to protect themselves. Eels are covered with slime. This makes them slippery and hard to catch. Porcupine fish, lionfish, stingrays, and scorpion fish are covered with sharp spikes. Puffer fish can blow up their bodies like a balloon to scare away predators.

Some fish don't have to worry about predators. They *are* the predators! Sharks, barracudas, and piranhas are a few fierce fish.

Stonefish

What's for Dinner? 4

If you have a goldfish or other fishy pet, you probably drop flakes of food in its tank every day. But no one feeds fish in the wild. So what do these fish eat?

Meat on the Menu

Most fish eat the meat of other animals. Worms, shrimp, squid, snails, and insects are tasty fish food. Large fish feast on smaller fish and other water creatures.

Emperor angelfish and parrot fish eat corals. Corals are small ocean animals that live in groups. Parrot fish use their hard beaks to scrape corals off rocks.

Emperor angelfish

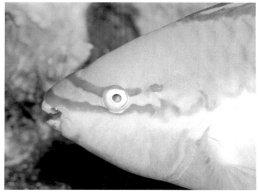

Princess parrot fish

17

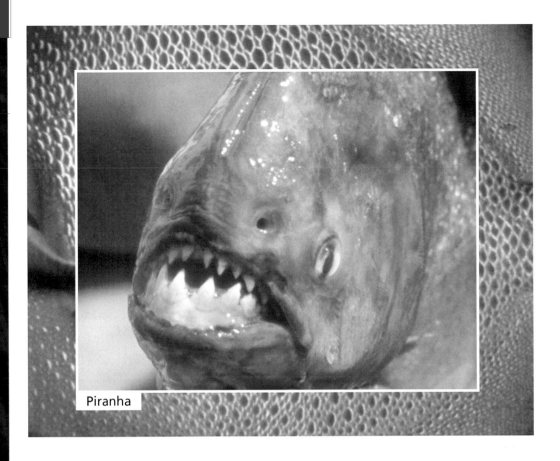
Piranha

Meat-eaters have many clever ways of catching their food. Rays, skates, and jewfish hide and then ambush prey. Schools of piranhas overtake their prey and use small teeth to tear off all the meat in minutes. The remora, or shark sucker, attaches itself to a shark's body and feasts on its leftovers. Swordfish injure other fish with a long, sharp bill. Anglerfish have special lures on their heads to attract prey.

Filter Food

Plankton are another treat for a variety of fish. Plankton are tiny **organisms** that live in the water. Fish eat plankton by opening their mouths wide to let in water containing plankton. The fish have special structures in their mouths to filter the plankton out of the water. This is called *filter feeding*.

Inquire and Investigate: Filter Feeding

Question: How are objects filtered out of water?

Answer the question: I think objects are filtered out of water when _____.

Form a hypothesis: Objects are filtered out of water when _____.

Test the hypothesis:

Materials
1 cup of gravel
1 cup of dirt
1 cup of sand
5 cups of water
2 buckets
several kitchen strainers with different-sized holes

Procedure
Fill one bucket with the gravel, dirt, sand, and water. Pour the mixture through a strainer into the second bucket. What materials are caught in the strainer? Repeat the procedure using each of the strainers. Record which materials are caught by each of the strainers. Note the size of the holes in each strainer.

Observations: Depending on the size of the holes in the strainer, it will catch different-sized pieces of rock, dirt, and sand. Much of the material may pass through a strainer with larger holes, while little or none of the materials may pass through a strainer with tiny holes.

Conclusions: Objects are filtered out of water when the water flows through instruments that catch objects of different sizes and let the water pass through. Fish filter food from water by straining it through their mouths. Special structures in their mouths catch the food while letting the water and other materials pass through.

Other Underwater Snacks

A few fish prefer plants. Many varieties of tilapia, carp, and angelfish are plant-eaters. Yellow tang fish eat wild grasses.

Algae are another fish snack. Algae are organisms that make their own food. Seaweed is one type of alga. Catfish, pupfish, and damselfish eat algae. Chinese algae eaters are named for their food of choice. Siamese algae eaters are the only fish known to eat red algae.

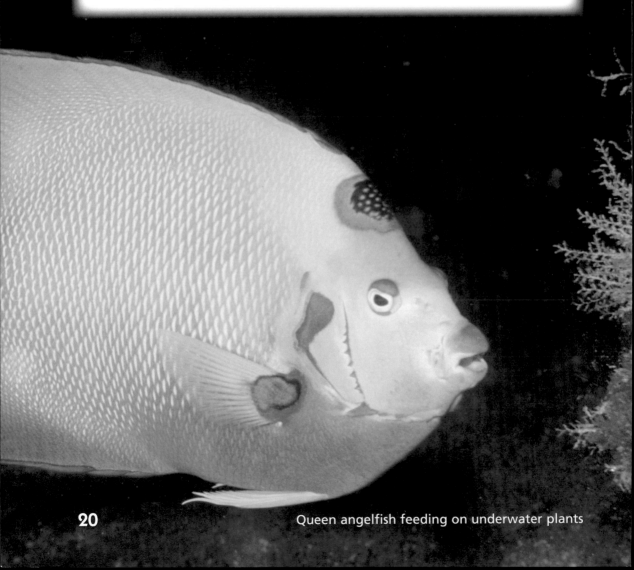

Queen angelfish feeding on underwater plants

Hanging Out 5

All fish live in water. But that water can be fresh or salty. It can be light or dark. It can also be hot or cold. Each kind of fish adapts to the type of water it calls home.

Fresh or Salty

About 40 percent of fish species live in freshwater. Freshwater habitats include lakes, rivers, and streams. Catfish, gar, perch, and lake trout are examples of freshwater fish.

Almost 60 percent of fish live in the salty water of the oceans. Sharks, marlins, groupers, and snappers are saltwater fish.

White marlin

A few species live in brackish water, which is a mixture of freshwater and salt water. Brackish water is often found in areas where the ocean meets the land. Archerfish, needlefish, puffer fish, mudskippers, and scats can live in brackish water.

Some fish spend part of their lives in freshwater and part of their lives in salt water. Salmon hatch in freshwater rivers. Then the fish swim out to the ocean. They live in the salty water until it's time for the females to lay eggs. Then the salmon swim back to the freshwater where they were born.

Other fish do just the opposite of salmon. Most eels are born in salt water. Then they swim to freshwater to live. When it's time to lay their eggs, the eels return to the ocean.

Puffer fish

Light or Dark

Most saltwater fish live near the top of the ocean. This area receives light and heat from the Sun. The sunlight makes **photosynthesis** possible, so there is plenty of food for the fish to eat. Tunas, stingrays, clown fish, and mackerels are among the fish that swim near the surface.

Other fish live deeper in the ocean where it's dark and cold. Food is scarce. Large eyes, big stomachs, and other features help fish survive here. Hatchet and viper fish have big eyes. Anglerfish and some eels have huge stomachs that can hold large amounts food when it's available.

Gold-spotted eel

Some deep-sea fish can produce their own light. This is called *bioluminescence*. Lantern fish and black dragonfish have rows of lights along their bodies. Cookiecutter and lantern sharks have glowing bellies. Fish use these lights to help them spot prey and find food and **mates**. Sometimes they even use the lights to trick prey into coming closer.

Lantern shark

Tropical or Frozen

Many fish live in the warm tropical waters near the equator. More species of freshwater fish swim in the tropics in Asia, Africa, and South America than any other place in the world. Puffer fish, parrot fish, swordfish, lionfish, and manta rays are common tropical fish.

Other fish live in cold waters. Sturgeon live in lakes and rivers in northern Europe, North America, and Russia. Cod and wolf fish live in the cold waters of the North Atlantic. Salmon and trout also prefer colder waters.

A few fish can even live in the freezing waters off Antarctica! The Antarctic cod and ice fish are two fish that brave the cold. These fish have special "antifreeze" chemicals in their blood that keep it from freezing.

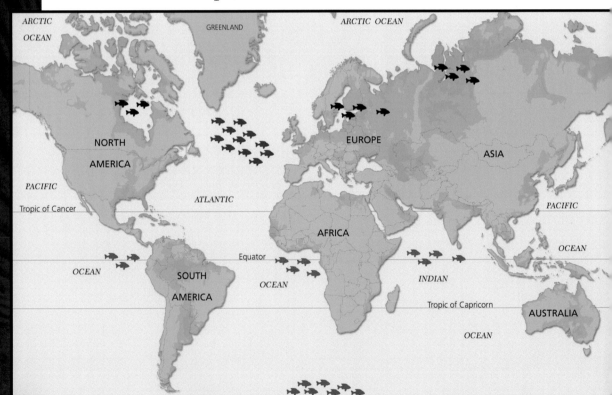

Puffer fish, parrot fish, swordfish, lionfish, and manta rays
Sturgeon, salmon, and trout
Cod, wolf fish, salmon, and trout
Antarctic cod and ice fish

What's Up with Fish?

6

  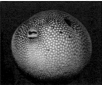  

It may seem as if there are plenty of fish in the sea. But are there really? Fish face many dangers in their underwater lives.

Something Is Fishy

People have caught fish for food for thousands of years. However, the huge commercial **fisheries** that have developed over the past 100 years have severely damaged many fish populations. For example, until recently, cod fishing was a major industry in the North Atlantic. At one time, 400 million fish were caught there every year.

But so many cod were taken from the water that eventually there weren't enough left to support the fishing industry.

Shrinking Fish

Overfishing has affected the size of North Atlantic cod. In the past, cod weighing up to 200 pounds were common. Today, a 40-pound cod is considered a big fish.

Anglers holding a 65-pound white marlin

Fishing for sport has also decreased the number of fish in our waters. At one time, fishing was unrestricted. People could catch and keep fish of any size or species. When too many small fish were caught, there weren't enough fish left to grow up and lay eggs for new fish. This decreased many fish populations.

What Happened to My Habitat?

Fish suffer when their habitats change or disappear. When people build shopping centers, houses, and businesses, they often fill in or redirect bodies of water. Salmon, for instance, always swim back to the rivers where they were born to lay their eggs. Today, however, their paths are often blocked by **dams**. If salmon can't get past a dam, they can't reproduce.

Water pollution is also a threat to fish. Oil, chemicals, pesticides, and garbage pollute water. These substances can poison fish or injure them in other ways. They can also reduce the amount of oxygen in the water, making it difficult for fish to breathe.

Few people have heard of Emmeline Moore. But this scientist was one of the first to study fish habitats.

Emmeline Moore was born in New York State in 1877. At that time, few careers were open to women. Like many others, Moore became a teacher. In the summers, however, she worked as an investigator for the U.S. Bureau of Fisheries. As part of this job, Moore traveled around New York counting and studying fish. She enjoyed this work so much that she eventually left teaching to work for the Bureau of Fisheries full-time.

In 1920, Moore became the first woman biologist for the New York State Department of Conservation. She studied and wrote reports on the characteristics and fish populations of lakes throughout the state. In 1949, New York passed a water pollution control law. Moore's reports were used to monitor the law's progress.

Moore became the director of New York State's Biological Survey in 1932. Her research took her all over the globe. Although she is not world famous, Moore is still remembered as one of the first scientists to study the environment and its effect on fish populations.

Sink or Swim

Efforts are being made to save threatened fish species. Governments around the world have set guidelines for fishing. These guidelines include how many fish of certain species can be caught and the size of fish that can be kept. Catch-and-release programs allow people to catch fish as long as they return them unharmed to the water. These guidelines are designed to protect fish populations while still allowing people to fish for food and sport.

Restocking fish habitats has also helped to increase the fish population. In the United States, the Department of Environmental Conservation raises millions of fish every year. These fish are then placed in streams, rivers, lakes, and ponds all over the country.

Technology Link

Fish hatcheries are places where fish are raised and studied by scientists. Then the fish are released into waters around the world to maintain populations and provide fish for recreational purposes.

How does a hatchery work? Adult fish are caught and brought to a hatchery. Here eggs are collected and **fertilized.** The eggs are then placed in hatching jars where the temperature is carefully controlled. After they hatch, the young fish swim into special tanks. Scientists monitor the fishes' growth. The water is constantly cleaned and kept at the right temperature. The fish are fed tiny creatures called *brine shrimp* and other foods specially designed to make them strong and healthy. When the fish are able to survive on their own, they are released back into natural waters.

Fish hatcheries are a great example of how science and technology can help nature regain some of the balance that human interference has destroyed.

Fish ladders have been built to help salmon. When a dam blocks a waterway used by salmon, these ladders offer the fish a way around the dam.

Governments have also passed laws to reduce water pollution. Companies that disobey these laws can be fined large sums of money and be forced to clean up the waterways.

Laws, guidelines, technology, and individual responsibility can help save a lot of our fish friends. By protecting the fish population, we ensure that our waters will remain full of life.

Fish ladder

Internet Connections and Related Reading for Fish

http://www.zoomschool.com/subjects/fish/printouts/
Dive into the fascinating world of fish with the information and animal printouts found here.

http://fishnkids.dpi.nsw.gov.au/
Learn fun fish facts, find out how to help save endangered fish, and complete other fishy activities at this "fish 'n' kids" site.

http://www.flmnh.ufl.edu/fish/Kids/kids.htm
Want to learn more about ichthyology (the study of fish)? Begin here with the student-friendly information on the characteristics of fish.

http://www.nefsc.noaa.gov/faq/
Get the answers to all of your questions about fish from this long list of frequently asked fish questions.

http://www.seaworld.org/wild-world/safari/virtual-aquarium/index.htm
Go on an aquatic safari to learn more about several species of fish.

Queen triggerfish

* * * * * * *

Amazing Fish by Mary Ling. Photographs and text describe amazing members of the fish family. Kids Can Press, 1991. [RL 4 IL 1–5] (4264501 PB)

Classifying Fish by Louise and Richard Spilsbury. Explains what fish are and how they differ from other animals. Heinemann Library, 2003. [RL 3 IL 3–5] (3453901 PB)

Fish Farms by Lynn Stone. Introduces the characteristics and habits of some fish species and how they are raised on farms. Rourke Book Company, Inc., 1999. [RL 4 IL 1–4] (3806406 HB)

Fish That Play Tricks by D. M. Souza. Describes the physical characteristics and behavior of such fish as the trumpetfish, grouper, parrot fish, and wrasse. Lerner, 1998. [RL 5.3 IL 3–7] (5994606 HB)

Fishes by Melissa Stewart. This book describes the basic behavior and physical traits of fish. Crabtree Publishing, 2001. [RL 3 IL 3–5] (6886701 PB 6886706 HB)

What's It Like to Be a Fish? by Wendy Pfeffer. Explains how a fish's body is perfectly suited to life underwater. HarperCollins, 1996. [RL 2 IL K–4] (4953301 PB 4953302 CC)

•RL = Reading Level
•IL = Interest Level

Perfection Learning's catalog numbers are included for your ordering convenience.
PB indicates paperback. CC indicates Cover Craft. HB indicates hardback.

Glossary

camouflage (KAM uh flahz) protective coloring or other characteristics that help animals hide from predators or prey (see separate entries for *predator* and *prey*)

cartilage (KAR tuh lidj) tough elastic tissue in an animal's body

dam (dam) barrier built across a river to control the flow of water

fertilize (FER tuh leyez) to bring male and female cells together to produce new organisms (see separate entry for *organism*)

fin (fin) flexible body part that fish use to balance and move through water

fishery (FISH er ee) business that catches, processes, and/or sells fish

gill (gil) body part that fish use to breathe underwater

habitat (HAB i tat) place where a plant or animal lives

mate (mayt) partner for reproduction (see separate entry for *reproduce*)

membrane (MEM brayn) thin, flexible sheet of tissue in living things that can connect or cover parts of the body

organism (OR guh niz uhm) living thing

photosynthesis (foh toh SIN thuh sis) process by which plants use energy from the Sun to make food

predator (PRED uh ter) animal that hunts other animals for food

prey (pray) animal that is hunted by other animals for food

reproduce (REE pruh doos) to make more members of the same species (see separate entry for *species*)

scale (skayl) one of many small, flat, stiff plates that cover a fish

species (SPEE shees) group of living things that resemble one another and can reproduce (see separate entry for *reproduce*)

swim bladder (swim BLAD er) air sac that draws in or releases air so a fish can move up and down in the water; also called an *air bladder* or *gas bladder.*

Blue ribbon eel

Index

Blenny